SPACESHIPS

BY JOHN HAMILTON

VISIT US AT

WWW.ABDOPUBLISHING.COM

Published by ABDO Publishing Company, 4940 Viking Drive, Suite 622, Edina, Minnesota 55435.
Copyright ©2007 by Abdo Consulting Group, Inc. International copyrights reserved in all countries.
No part of this book may be reproduced in any form without written permission from the publisher.
ABDO & Daughters™ is a trademark and logo of ABDO Publishing Company.

Printed in the United States.

Editor: Paul Joseph
Graphic Design: John Hamilton
Cover Design: Neil Klinepier
Cover Illustration: *White Wing* ©1984 Janny Wurts
Interior Photos and Illustrations: p 1 *Hellburner* ©1992 Don Maitz; p 4 astronauts spacewalking,
Corbis; p 5 *Entering Saturn's Rings* ©1977 Don Maitz; p 6 scene from *A Trip to the Moon*, Corbis;
p 7 *Apollo 11* liftoff, NASA; p 8 scene from *2001: A Space Odyssey*, Getty Images; p 9 *White Wing* ©1984
Janny Wurts; p 10 Space Shuttle main engine test, NASA; p 11 *Far Traveler* ©1977 Don Maitz; p 12
Space Shuttle flight deck, NASA; p 13 *In the Oceans of Venus* ©1977 Don Maitz; p 14 International Space
Station, NASA; p 15 *Shuttle Run* ©1978 Janny Wurts; p 16 *Solo* ©1985 Janny Wurts; p 17 Moon base,
NASA; p 18 spaceship, NASA; p 19 astronaut on Mars, NASA; p 20 *Landfall* ©1979 Janny Wurts; p 21
cloud of ionized gas, NASA; p 22 space ark, NASA; p 23 *Cryogenesis* ©1983 Janny Wurts; p 24 *Empire
Fleet Transport* ©1977 Don Maitz; p 25 *The Probe* ©1976 Don Maitz; p 26 Galaxy PKS 0521-36, NASA;
p 27 *Attack on Pell Station*, ©1983 Janny Wurts; p 28 (top) starship *Enterprise*, Corbis; p 28 (bottom left)
mother ship, *Close Encounters of the Third Kind*, courtesy Columbia Pictures; p 28 (bottom right) Death
Star, courtesy 20th Century Fox; p 29 (upper left) *Millennium Falcon*, NASA (background); p 29 (upper
right) Borg Cube, courtesy Paramount Pictures; p 29 (lower left) lobby poster for *2001: A Space Odyssey*,
courtesy MGM; p 29 (lower right) Martian cylinder, Corbis; p 30 *Rimrunners* ©1988 Don Maitz; p 32
Apollo 11 in orbit around Moon, NASA.

Library of Congress Cataloging-in-Publication Data

Hamilton, John, 1959-
  Spaceships / John Hamilton.
    p. cm. -- (The world of science fiction)
  Includes bibliographical references and index.
  ISBN-13: 978-1-59679-995-0
  ISBN-10: 1-59679-995-1
  1. Interplanetary voyages--Juvenile literature. 2. Space vehicles--Juvenile literature. 3. Science
fiction--History and criticism--Juvenile literature. I. Title. II. Series.

TL793.H3425 2007
629.45--dc22
                          2006007269

CONTENTS

TO THE STARS

Spaceships are the most common way for science fiction heroes to travel to the stars, and beyond. In fact, spaceships naturally come to mind when most people think of science fiction. Silver rockets whizzing past the stars, flying saucers whirling in the sky, giant starships lifting off from distant planets—spaceships combine gee-whiz science with fantastic adventure, the very hallmark of good science fiction.

Science fiction is about exploring frontiers. Like cowboys who venture onto wide-open ranges, science fiction characters go to strange new worlds, where they meet unexpected challenges. In these faraway places, there is no hope of rescue or outside assistance—the distance from home is too great. That makes for good storytelling, because the best stories are the ones where heroes must fix problems on their own.

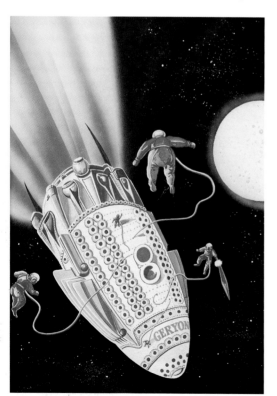

For decades, science fiction authors have dreamed up bold new designs to transport astronauts from one star to the next. Early spaceship designs were often fantastic and far-fetched, like bullet-shaped capsules shot out of giant cannons. Others were surprisingly realistic. A 1929 issue of editor Hugo Gernsback's *Science Wonder Quarterly* showed a trio of spacewalking astronauts tethered to their accurate-looking ship, decades before Gemini and Apollo astronauts went into space.

Left: Frank R. Paul painted this scene of three spacewalking astronauts for the first issue of Hugo Gernsback's *Science Wonder Quarterly* in 1929. The image at left was meticulously recreated by artist Anton Brzezinski.
Facing page: Entering Saturn's Rings, by Don Maitz.

Science fiction writers have a talent for accurately predicting the future. Arthur C. Clarke, author of *2001: A Space Odyssey*, wrote scientifically accurate stories about man-made satellites many years before they became a reality.

Author Ben Bova, chairman of the National Space Society Board, once wrote, "Science fiction is not only the best way to predict the future, it has also helped to create the civilian space program. Name any other method of attempting to forecast the future... including the work of professional scientists.... Read their predictions five or ten years after they were written. Pitiful! Science fiction writers, on the other hand, have predicted virtually every aspect of our modern world—often 30 or more years before the events came to pass."

In 1865, French author Jules Verne wrote *From the Earth to the Moon*. The story was about people who built an enormous cannon that fired a spaceship to the moon. Verne actually tried to figure out how big the cannon would have to be in order to provide enough force for the mission. Writing almost 100 years before today's space program, Verne made many uncannily accurate predictions.

Verne's spaceship contained three people, just like the Apollo spacecraft that took American astronauts to the moon. Verne named his spaceship *Columbiad*. Apollo 11's command module was named *Columbia*. Verne described the weightlessness that astronauts would feel. Also, his fictional spaceship blasted off from Florida, just like most of NASA's spaceships. These and other similarities to today's spacecraft proved that Verne was a very forward-thinking science fiction writer.

Facing page: The *Apollo 11* spacecraft blasts off for the moon on July 16, 1969.
Below: The Man in the Moon gets hit in the eye by a spaceship in this scene from *A Trip to the Moon*. The 1902 silent film by Georges Méliès was inspired in part by Jules Verne's story, *From the Earth to the Moon*.

Sometimes, however, scientific accuracy isn't the point of a good science fiction story. In 1901, H. G. Wells wrote *The First Men in the Moon*. To get his astronauts into space, Wells dreamed up a substance called Cavorite, which cancelled the effects of gravity.

Jules Verne was annoyed that Wells could get away with such a fanciful invention. Verne complained that Wells' book wasn't science, it was pure fantasy. In 1903, he told an interviewer, "I do not see the possibility of comparison between his work and mine.... I make use of physics. He invents. I go to the moon in a cannonball, discharged from a cannon. Here there is no invention. He goes [to the moon] in an airship, which he constructs of a metal which does away with the law of gravitation."

What Verne failed to see was that Wells didn't really care *how* his characters got to the moon—that wasn't the point of his story. Instead, Wells wanted to tell about what his astronauts found *after* they landed on the moon. Jules Verne's story, on the other hand, was mostly about the adventure of the journey itself. As the old saying goes, sometimes the thrill is in the journey, not the destination.

From the Earth to the Moon and *The First Men in the Moon* are two different kinds of science fiction stories. Science fiction today is often divided into these two groups. Some are filled with scientific detail—*hard science fiction*. On the other hand, *soft science fiction* focuses more on character and plot.

When science fiction authors or filmmakers create their spacecraft, they can choose to be scientifically accurate if realism is important to the story. *2001: A Space Odyssey* is famous for its realistic spaceships. But if action and adventure are more important to the story, then reality is often purposely ignored in order to heighten the mood. After all, how exciting would *Stars Wars* be without X-Wing fighters dodging laser cannons (very difficult to do without retro rockets) or blowing up Death Stars with loud explosions and fireballs (impossible in the vacuum of space)?

Facing page: White Wing, by Janny Wurts.
Below: A scene from *2001: A Space Odyssey.*

SHIP DESIGNS

For writers of hard science fiction, when realism is the goal, there are certain basic spaceship systems that must be included to make a story believable.

First, a ship needs some type of propulsion system. What kind of engines does the ship have, and what kind of fuel does it use? There are many possibilities, such as solid versus chemical rockets, or nuclear fuel, or technologies that haven't been invented yet, such as antimatter propulsion or solar-powered sails. Whatever propulsion system the sci fi writer uses, it has to make sense within the world he is creating. For example, a story about humans pioneering the solar system would probably describe propulsion systems similar to today's technology, such as liquid-fuel rockets. Only an advanced civilization would have exotic propulsion systems like anti-gravity or black-hole stardrives.

Guidance systems help steer spaceships. The laws of physics state that once an object is in motion, it will keep going until it meets some kind of resistance. On Earth, that resistance is usually gravity and air. But in space, once you get a spaceship moving, the only way to stop it is to apply a burst of power in the opposite direction. Today's spacecraft use retro-rockets and thrusters to maneuver. In realistic sci fi stories, spaceships use some kind of reverse thruster to slow down or make turns. In softer science fiction, such as *Star Wars*, spaceships behave much as airplanes do on Earth. They turn, bank, and dive as if they are sailing through the atmosphere, like jet fighters. In reality, in the cold vacuum of space, they could never move like this, unless some new kind of technology is discovered that uses invisible retro thrusters. Perhaps a kind of anti-motion machine?

Facing page: Far Traveler, by Don Maitz.
Below: Engineers at NASA test fire a Space Shuttle main engine.

The ship's interior is also important. It must have a cabin structure big enough and strong enough to support a crew for however long the journey lasts. The interior must have a proper life support system. The crew will need plenty of oxygen and water to survive. Will they bring it all with them, or will they save room by manufacturing materials during the trip? In some science fiction stories, huge containers of plants are grown in order to give the crew a steady supply of oxygen, which plants give off as part of their normal life cycle. Plants also absorb carbon dioxide, which humans exhale. Too much carbon dioxide is dangerous, so having some sort of air-filtering system, like plants, or at least air-scrubbing machines, is critical.

Some spaceship systems are often overlooked by writers, even in hard science fiction. A communications system is crucial to talk not only with the home planet and other ships, but also between the astronauts who might inhabit different parts of the ship. Thermal and radiation protection is critical to keep astronauts shielded from the cold, harsh conditions of space, which lurk just outside the thin hull of the ship. Lastly, displays and controls must be well thought out and easy to use. Many science fiction stories use standard video displays, while some use more exotic methods, such as telepathy.

Facing page: In the Oceans of Venus, by Don Maitz.
Below: Astronauts at work on the flight deck of the Space Shuttle *Atlantis.*

INTERPLANETARY TRAVEL

Interplanetary means to travel around or between the planets of our solar system. It's not as simple as it might seem. Compared to a journey to another planet, such as Mars, a trip to Earth's moon and back is relatively easy. The amount of fuel needed isn't that great, because Earth's gravity does much of the work. Still, even a trip this short can be extremely hazardous. The film *Apollo 13*, based on a true story, showed how quickly things can go wrong, and how difficult it is to get back home safely.

Mission planners will have to provide just the right amount of fuel for the return journey once a spaceship leaves the influence of Earth's gravity. Also, astronauts will require enough oxygen, food, and supplies for a trip that could last months, or even years. The astronauts will have to be self-sufficient; in case of an emergency, a rescue ship will never reach them in time.

An interplanetary journey might begin high above Earth. The ship would probably be large, in order to handle all of the fuel and supplies needed for the long trip. It would be much easier to build the spacecraft in the weightlessness of Earth orbit. The International Space Station (ISS) might be very handy for building such a large ship. It would be a long-term base where astronauts could live as they construct the spacecraft.

Right: Orbiting high above Earth, the International Space Station might make a good base for astronauts to construct a spaceship for an interplanetary journey.
Facing page: Shuttle Run, by Janny Wurts.

Just getting into orbit is difficult. It takes enormous rockets, such as those used on the Space Shuttle, to lift heavy loads into space. Right now, with today's technology, it might be too expensive to build the kind of ship needed to take a large crew to distant planets. The total cost of the ISS alone is $60-$100 billion, according to the U.S. government. No one knows exactly how much money it would cost to build an interplanetary spacecraft, but it will be frighteningly expensive by today's standards, unless new technologies are developed.

In his novel, *The Fountains of Paradise*, Arthur C. Clarke devised a much cheaper method of getting materials into space. Clarke imagined a kind of space elevator that would quickly whisk astronauts and materials into orbit. By using satellites in geosynchronous orbit (where the satellite stays in the same spot over the earth), elevators could be lowered to the ground by super-strong cables. Counterweights would be sent in the opposite direction, away from Earth, to keep the satellites' orbits stable. It's an exciting idea, and theoretically possible, but the technology to make it happen doesn't yet exist. But perhaps, someday, we'll be able to take an elevator ride into space!

Below: Solo, by Janny Wurts:

Given the difficulties, and the costs, why bother going to the planets at all? There are many good reasons. Our Earth has limited resources and a growing population. Some scientists estimate we only have 300 years left before we suffer critical shortages of water and fuel.

Space probes show that there are a wealth of minerals on the asteroids, planets, and moons of our own solar system. We need to find a way to safely travel to these distant places and mine the precious resources they contain.

Below: An artist's vision of what a future Moon base might look like.

Mining, commerce, and exploration will drive us into space. Otherwise, there will be a steady dwindling of Earth's resources, and a drastic change in how humans live. The worst-case scenario: total extinction. Unfortunately, with today's technology, the difficulties of manned space travel are many.

To overcome these hurdles, science fiction writers are constantly dreaming up new ideas to get us safely from one planet to another. Sometimes the ideas aren't so far-fetched, like Arthur C. Clarke's space elevator. Perhaps someday a new idea hatched by an author of science fiction will lead to a breakthrough in how people travel to other planets.

Facing page: An astronaut searches for minerals on Mars.
Below: A spaceship travels beyond the moons of Jupiter.

INTERSTELLAR TRAVEL

Using today's technology, a trip to another planet in our own solar system might take several months or a few years. Interstellar travel is a voyage between the stars. Such a trip would take perhaps thousands, or millions, of years. It depends on where in the universe, with all its infinite space, you want to go.

For the science fiction author, there are many good reasons to write about astronauts exploring new star systems and the worlds they contain. One reason is simply for the adventure, to explore places and alien societies that are completely different from Earth. In the early days of science fiction, authors often wrote about aliens on our neighboring planets, like Mars or Venus. But as we know today, unless a story is a total fantasy, finding aliens on Mars, or any other planet in our solar system, is impossible. NASA space probes have shown just how harsh and inhospitable the other planets really are. The only realistic places you might find aliens are on planets in other parts of the galaxy.

Facing page: A huge bubble of ionized gas and warm dust, called RCW 79, lies in the Milky Way Galaxy, thousands of light-years from Earth.
Below: Landfall, by Janny Wurts.

Unfortunately, interstellar travel presents a great dilemma: time. Although there are trillions upon trillions of stars in the universe, the distance between them is vast. Using today's space flight technology, it would take huge amounts of time to get from one star to another, much longer than a human lifespan.

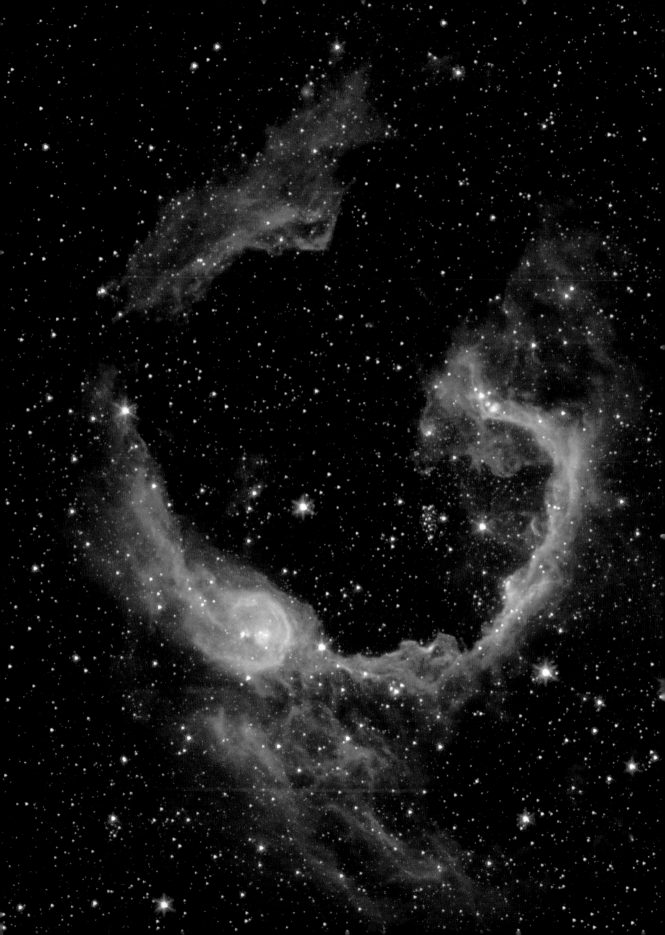

Why not just make a spaceship that can go super-fast? It can't be done, because there's a speed limit to the universe—the speed of light. Physicist Albert Einstein proved that nothing can go faster than light speed, which is approximately 186,282 miles per second (299,792 km/sec).

The closest star to Earth (besides the Sun) is Proxima Centauri, which is 4.3 light years away. A light year is the distance that light can travel in a year, which is approximately 5.9 trillion miles (9.5 trillion km). That means that even if you could invent a spaceship that travels close to the speed of light, it would still take almost nine years to make a trip there and back. And that's just to our closest star! There are trillions of stars in the universe many billions of times farther away.

Obviously, a story would be boring indeed if each trip to a new planet took thousands of years. How do science fiction authors get around the fact that interstellar distances are so vast? There are several ways, some of which are grounded in hard science, and some of which flirt with fantasy.

One science fiction solution is a generation spaceship. This is a ship big enough to hold a whole community of space explorers. Also called a space ark, a generation ship would travel to other star systems at sub-light speed, traveling perhaps hundreds of years to its destination. The astronauts would live their entire lives in the ship—through birth, childhood, school, adulthood, and ultimately, death. Plants would be grown in giant agricultural pods in order to provide food and oxygen. Water would be recycled. By the time the space ark reached its goal, several generations would have lived and died on the ship. It would be as if your great-grandparents started the journey, and you were the lucky ones to arrive at the destination to explore its wonders.

An alternative to a generation ship is to have the crew spend the voyage in some sort of suspended animation. The astronauts would be cryogenically frozen for the duration of the journey. Once the destination was reached, the ship's computer would automatically awaken the explorers.

Facing page: Cryogenesis, by artist Janny Wurts. *Below:* A NASA-designed space ark. Perhaps someday generations of space explorers will live in such a spacecraft.

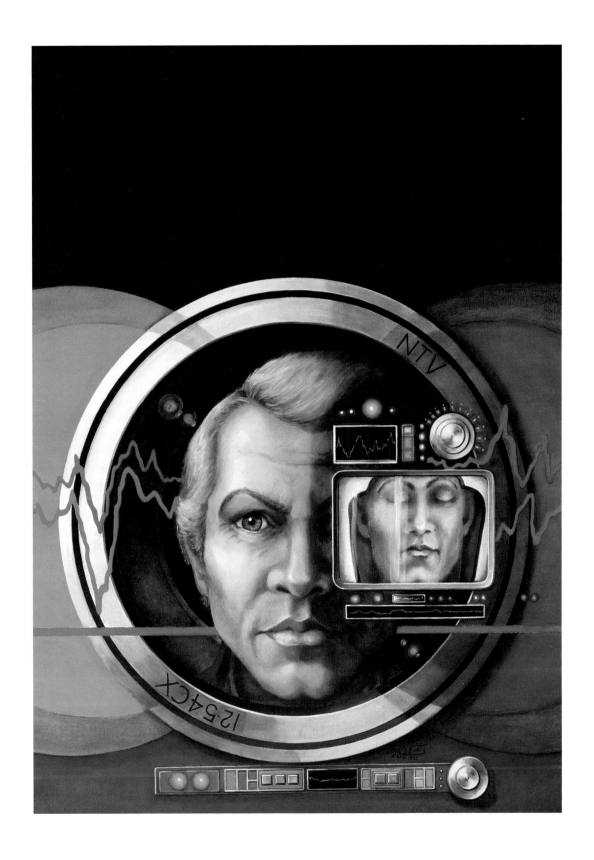

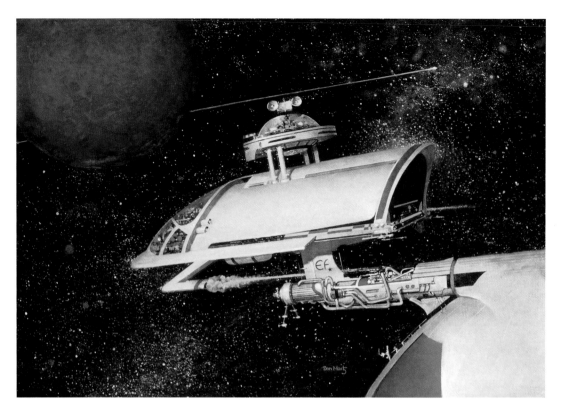

Above: Empire Fleet Transport, by Don Maitz.

In most science fiction, there's simply no other choice than to have characters travel to other star systems as rapidly as possible, and that means using spaceships that travel faster than light speed. Science fiction authors are clever people, and over the years they've dreamed up several ways to get around the light speed barrier.

One way to go faster than light is to devise a spaceship that uses hyperspace drives. According to science fiction author Orson Scott Card, in his excellent book, *How to Write Science Fiction & Fantasy*, the term hyperspace has been used by writers since the 1940s.

The universe that we're aware of exists in three dimensions (left to right, forward and backward, up and down). But what if there were other dimensions, and what if someday we could travel within them? And if a spaceship traveled through another dimension, what if normal three-dimensional space gets curved and warped, so that distant places are actually much closer to us? When we come out of hyperspace, it would be as if we had traveled faster than light.

Hyperspace is a bizarre concept. It's sometimes difficult to understand. Think of two points on opposite sides of a sheet of paper. Each point represents a star, normally too far apart for a spaceship to travel in between. But enter hyperspace, and the paper starts to fold in on itself, until the two points actually touch. Our fictional astronauts could leap, or "jump," from one point to another while in hyperspace, then return to normal three-dimensional space. To an observer who stays in three-dimensional space, the astronauts would appear to cross from one point to the other much faster than the speed of light!

Left: If interstellar flight proves too difficult, future missions will have to be flown by unmanned space vehicles, like this one from artist Don Maitz' *The Probe.*

Facing page: Assault on Pell Station, by Janny Wurts. *Below:* A NASA image of galaxy PKS 0521-36, based on data from the Hubble Space Telescope. The galaxy has a jet that spews gas and other material. These cosmic fireworks are probably caused by a massive, spinning black hole in the center of the galaxy. Could future astronauts harness this power to break the speed of light?

In Madeleine L'Engle's *A Wrinkle in Time,* the heroes break the speed of light by traveling through a tesseract, a kind of fifth dimension, very much like hyperspace. As Charles, one of the book's main characters, explained, "Well, the fifth dimension's a tesseract. You add that to the other four dimensions and you can travel through space without having to go the long way around. In other words… a straight line is *not* the shortest distance between two points."

Hyperspace travel sounds fanciful, but it may actually be possible. Wormholes are theoretical tunnels through time and space. Some physicists think these time/space tunnels may be very common, with links to distant galaxies, or even completely different universes! Wormholes have not yet been proven. And even if they do exist, nobody knows if a person could survive a passage through a wormhole. But the possibilities are mind-boggling, and creators of science fiction have seized upon the concept. Wormholes have appeared in many science fiction novels, movies, and television shows, including Carl Sagan's *Contact, Star Trek: Deep Space Nine, Stargate SG-1,* and Larry Niven and Jerry Pournelle's *The Mote in God's Eye.*

Of course, science fiction creators often dispense with the techno mumbo-jumbo, ignoring the light-speed problem

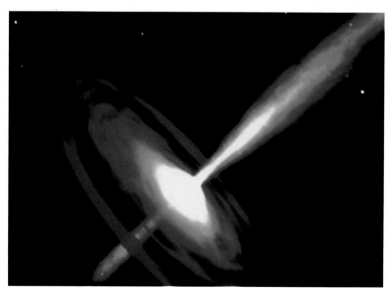

altogether. This has the advantage of focusing on plot and characters more than technical details. For example, the ships of *Star Trek* use "warp drives," which transport them to distant stars in mere days. It's not very good science, but it's a literary device that works well with adventure stories.

27

FAMOUS SF SPACECRAFT

USS *ENTERPRISE*
STAR TREK
TELEVISION AND FEATURE FILMS—1966-2005

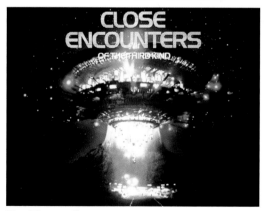

THE MOTHER SHIP
CLOSE ENCOUNTERS OF THE THIRD KIND
FEATURE FILM—1977

THE DEATH STAR
FEATURE FILMS—*STAR WARS* (1977); *RETURN OF
THE JEDI* (1983); *REVENGE OF THE SITH* (2005)

MILLENNIUM FALCON
FEATURE FILMS—STAR WARS (1977); THE EMPIRE STRIKES BACK (1980); RETURN OF THE JEDI (1983)

THE BORG CUBE
TELEVISION SERIES—STAR TREK: THE NEXT GENERATION (1987-1994); STAR TREK: VOYAGER (1995-2001)
FEATURE FILM—STAR TREK: FIRST CONTACT (1996)

SPACE STATION & SPACESHIP DISCOVERY ONE
FEATURE FILM—2001: A SPACE ODYSSEY (1968)

THE MARTIAN CYLINDERS
NOVEL—THE WAR OF THE WORLDS (1898), BY H. G. WELLS.

GLOSSARY

ANTIMATTER

A kind of matter that has the exact opposite electrical charge as matter found in our universe. If a piece of matter and antimatter collided, pure energy would be released. Some scientists speculate that it may be possible to open a kind of "window" into alternate universes where antimatter exists. If antimatter could somehow be contained and harnessed, it could be used as a clean and efficient fuel for future spaceships.

GALAXY

A system of millions, or even hundreds of billions, of stars and planets, clustered together in a distinct shape, like a spiral or ellipse. Our Earth is located within the Milky Way Galaxy.

GEOSYNCHRONOUS ORBIT

A satellite that orbits a planet at the same rate that the planet revolves around its axis. In effect, the satellite stays over the same spot of the planet's surface.

HARD SCIENCE FICTION

Science fiction that emphasizes facts and reality. Hard science fiction is filled with scientific detail. It tries to present a realistic speculation of how science will affect future societies.

HYPERSPACE

A kind of space that exists in theory (and in many science fiction stories) in which a craft can travel faster than the speed of light.

Left: Rimrunners, by Don Maitz.

INTERPLANETARY
To travel around or between the planets of our solar system. A journey from Earth to Mars would be an interplanetary trip.

INTERSTELLAR
Something that happens or exists between the stars of a galaxy. A rocketship that travels through interstellar space is moving from one star system to the next.

LIGHT YEAR
The distance light travels in a year, approximately 5.9 trillion miles (9.5 trillion km).

NASA
The National Aeronautics and Space Administration. NASA is the United States' main space agency, responsible for programs such as the Space Shuttle and unmanned space probes.

SOFT SCIENCE FICTION
Science fiction that emphasizes plot and characters more than scientific detail and realism. Space operas such as *Star Wars* are often considered soft science fiction. For example, *Star Wars* space battles feature noisy and fiery explosions, impossible in the airless vacuum of space.

SOLAR SYSTEM
The collection of planets, asteroids, and comets that orbit the Sun. The solar system includes nine recognized planets: Mercury, Venus, Earth, Mars, Jupiter, Saturn, Uranus, Neptune, and Pluto.

TELEPATHY
The communication of thoughts or ideas by means other than the known senses. Often called "mind reading."

INDEX

Below: Apollo 11 in orbit
around the Moon, July 20,
1969.

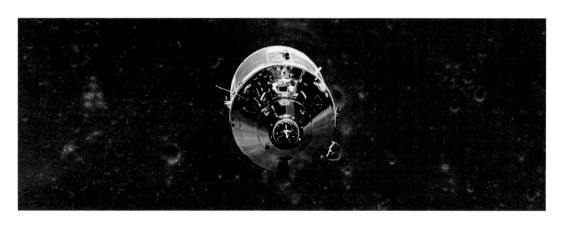

THE HUMAN MACHINE

DIGESTION AND EXCRETION

Louise Spilsbury

612.3
SPILSBURY, L

© 2008 Heinemann Library
a division of Reed Elsevier Inc.
Chicago, Illinois

Customer Service 888-454-2279
Visit our website at www.heinemannraintree.com

Designed by Victoria Bevan and AMR Design Ltd
Illustrations by Medi-mation
Picture Research by Hannah Taylor

Originated by Chroma
Printed and bound in China by CTPS

12 11 10 09 08
10 9 8 7 6 5 4 3 2 1

**Library of Congress Cataloging-in-Publication
Data**

Spilsbury, Louise.
  Digestion and excretion / Louise Spilsbury.
      p. cm. -- (The human machine)
  Includes index.
  ISBN-13: 978-1-4329-0905-5 (hardback : alk.
paper)
  ISBN-13: 978-1-4329-0912-3 (pbk. : alk. paper)
  1. Digestion--Juvenile literature. 2. Excretion--
Juvenile literature. I. Title.
  QP145.S72 2007
  612.3--dc22

                        2007031965

Acknowledgments
The publishers would like to thank the following
for permission to reproduce photographs: ©Corbis
pp. **9** (Royalty Free), **26** (Envision), **19** (Lester
Lefkowitz), **16** (Roy Morsch), **10** (zefa/ Alexander
Scott); ©Getty Images pp. **23**, **20** (Datacraft),
4 (Photodisc), **15** (Photographer's Choice), **5**
(Stone +); ©iStockphoto p. **29** (Justin Horrocks),
©Masterfile p. **8** (John Lee); ©Photolibrary.com
pp. **7**, **25** (Stockbyte); ©Science Photo Library pp.
27 (AJ Photo), **17** (Alex Bartel), **12** (Eye of Science),
28 (Roger Harris).

Cover photograph of transparent male body
containing the digestive system reproduced with
permission of ©Getty Images/ 3D4Medical.com.

The publishers would like to thank David Wright
for his assistance in the preparation of this book.

Contents

Any words appearing in the text in bold, **like this**, are explained in the glossary.

What Is Digestion?

The human body is often described as a complex machine, because it is made up of many different parts that work together. To make machines work, you need a source of **energy**. Computers and MP3 players run on electricity, and cars and airplanes run on gasoline or diesel fuel. The human machine runs on a variety of different food fuels, including breads and pasta, fruits and vegetables, and meats, nuts, and cheese.

Digesting food

The body cannot use the food we take into our mouths as it is. To use food, your body must first **digest** it, or break it down. Inside the body, the different parts of the digestive system process the food. They break it down until it **dissolves** into incredibly tiny pieces in liquid. The **nutrients** in this liquid give the human machine the energy it needs to live. They also supply the raw materials the body uses to grow and repair any damage.

Today some cars run on ethanol, a kind of fuel made from corn oil. This means that the same corn plants can be used to run vehicles as well as human "engines"!

We cook some types of food, such as spaghetti, to make them easier for the body to digest. Cooking also changes the taste and appearance of food.

Waste not, want not

Some of the parts of the food we take in are not useful and could even be bad for us. The excretory system helps us to stay healthy by **excreting** (forcing out) wastes that could build up and make us sick. Unwanted parts of food and other food wastes pass from the digestive system to the excretory system and out of the body. After you have eaten a meal, your body is hard at work processing that fuel for up to 24 hours. The food passes through many different body parts on its long journey!

FAVORITE PLANT FOODS

There are more than 50,000 different plants that people can eat. However, just three of them—rice, maize (corn), and wheat—provide 60 percent of the world's food energy intake! People grow fields of these plants all around the world and often eat them for most meals. However, these plants do not provide all the nutrients people need.

What Are the Parts of the Digestive System?

The digestive system is like a conveyor belt in a factory. It consists mostly of a long tube made of several different **organs**. (Organs are body parts with a particular job to do.) This long tube is called the **alimentary canal**. Food passing through this tube is processed and sorted into useful nutrients the body wants and waste it does not want. It is similar to the way a juicing machine separates out the part of the fruit you can drink.

The stomach

From the mouth, food passes down the throat into the **esophagus**. The esophagus is a soft, **muscular** tube that is up to 12 inches (30 centimeters) long. It moves food to the stomach. The stomach is an organ that is like a stretchy bag. It holds up to 2 pints (1 liter) of food that a person has recently eaten. The stomach is about 6 inches (15 centimeters) wide at its widest point.

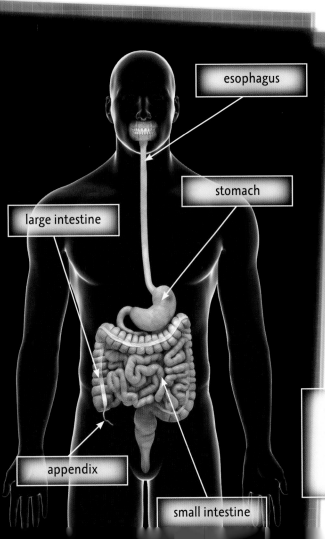

esophagus

stomach

large intestine

appendix

small intestine

This is the alimentary canal. It is mostly coiled up, but if stretched out it would measure 30 feet (9 meters) long in an adult. That is the length of a large bus!

The digestive system works like this juicing machine. It allows the body to separate off the parts of food that are good for us, such as apple juice, from the waste we do not want, such as seeds and skin.

The intestines

From the stomach, the partly digested food passes into the **small intestine**. This coiled, narrow tube makes up around two-thirds of the total length of the alimentary canal. It is where most digestion occurs. Undigested food and some water travels to the **large intestine**, which breaks down food remains and then passes waste out of the **anus**.

A SPARE PART

Our digestive system has an extra part on the large intestine called the appendix. Scientists think that in the past the appendix might have helped humans to digest tough, woody plant foods. Today it does not have a particular job because we eat more cooked foods. Therefore, if it gets infected it is sometimes removed altogether.

How Is Food Digested?

The process of digestion starts before you take your first bite of food. When you see a dish of delicious dinner or smell something simmering in the kitchen, your salivary glands start to work. The salivary glands are under the tongue. They produce saliva, or spit, which moistens food and makes it softer. Saliva also contains **enzymes**, which are chemicals that start to break down the food.

Tongue tactics

Your tongue is another part of the human machine that helps with digestion. It moves food around your mouth to spread the saliva. It also moves the food toward the back teeth so they can grind up the food. The tongue is covered in taste buds. Taste buds do an important job in digestion by warning us if food has gone bad as well as letting us taste food flavors.

The expression "makes your mouth water" is not far off, because the sight and smell of food does stimulate your salivary glands!

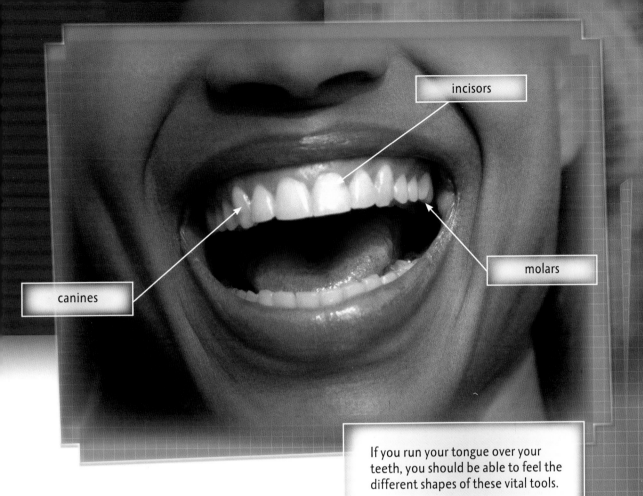

incisors

canines

molars

If you run your tongue over your teeth, you should be able to feel the different shapes of these vital tools.

Biting and chewing

Your teeth are like different tools. They are different shapes because they have different jobs to do. The four front teeth are incisors. They have straight, flat ends that bite through food so we can take a piece into our mouth. On each side of the incisors are long, sharp, and pointed canine teeth that grip and tear off pieces of tough food. At the back of your mouth are wide, flat-topped molars. These teeth are used for crushing, grinding, and chewing.

CHEMICAL DEMOLITION GANGS

Enzymes in the saliva start to digest **carbohydrates**. Carbohydrates are foods such as cereals, potatoes, breads, and pasta. The enzymes soak into the food and change the surface so it starts to break up into pieces of **glucose**. Glucose is a kind of sugar, which is why bread starts to taste a little sweet after you have been chewing it for a few minutes.

Swallowing

Together, the teeth and tongue shape the chewed food into a ball. Then, you use your throat to swallow the ball. The throat is made of two pipes. The esophagus takes food to the stomach, and the trachea takes air to the **lungs**. A flap of skin called the **epiglottis** normally closes like a trapdoor to make sure food only goes into the esophagus. If the epiglottis does not have enough time to close, food gets into the trachea. This makes you automatically choke or cough to clear the airway.

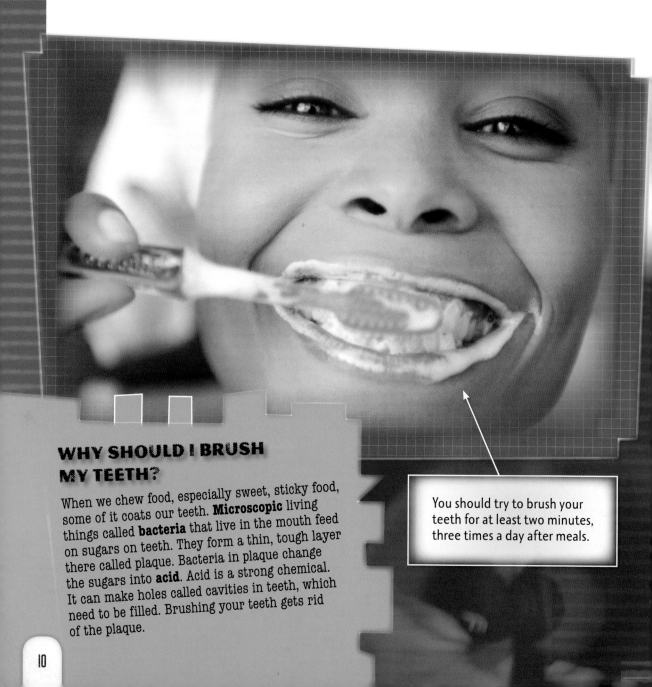

You should try to brush your teeth for at least two minutes, three times a day after meals.

WHY SHOULD I BRUSH MY TEETH?

When we chew food, especially sweet, sticky food, some of it coats our teeth. **Microscopic** living things called **bacteria** that live in the mouth feed on sugars on teeth. They form a thin, tough layer there called plaque. Bacteria in plaque change the sugars into **acid**. Acid is a strong chemical. It can make holes called cavities in teeth, which need to be filled. Brushing your teeth gets rid of the plaque.

Muscles in action

The walls of the alimentary canal have **muscles** all the way along them. These muscles squeeze the food through the esophagus after it leaves the throat. The food moves along the tube in the same way toothpaste moves when you squeeze the tube. The muscles in the esophagus are quite strong, and they can keep your food going in the right direction even if you eat upside down—although this is not recommended!

Into the stomach

When food passes into the stomach, a ring of muscle at the end of the esophagus squeezes tightly to stop the food from getting out again. When you swallow food or liquid, you also swallow air into the stomach. The air we breathe contains gases that you need to get rid of. This gas is sometimes forced out of the stomach, up through the esophagus, and out of your mouth as a burp.

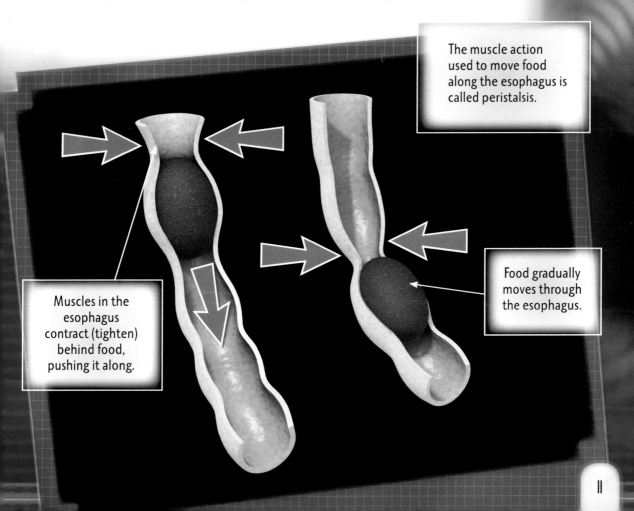

The muscle action used to move food along the esophagus is called peristalsis.

Muscles in the esophagus contract (tighten) behind food, pushing it along.

Food gradually moves through the esophagus.

The food processor

The stomach is like a food processor that turns lumps of food into a mushy mixture called **chyme**. The walls of the stomach have strong muscles that squeeze and churn the food inside, mixing and mashing it together. The stomach walls also release gastric juice. This contains strong acids to kill bacteria in food we have eaten that could otherwise make us sick. It also contains enzymes to break down **proteins**. Digestion in the stomach takes up to six hours, depending on the types of food we have eaten. For example, it takes longer to digest meat than bread.

Into the small intestine

Chyme moves from the stomach into the small intestine through a small flap. It then stays in the small intestine for about four hours while it is digested further. The small intestine is only about 1 inch (2.5 centimeters) wide. It is lined with thousands of microscopic **villi**, which are tiny folds that look like fingers. They stick out of the walls of the small intestine, pointing toward the center.

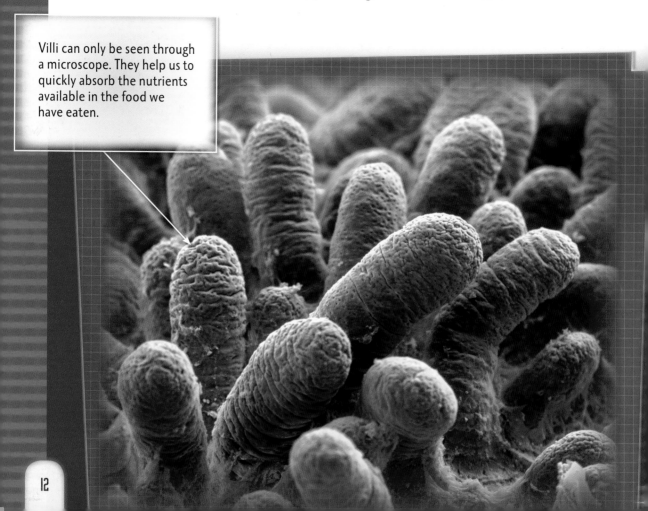

Villi can only be seen through a microscope. They help us to quickly absorb the nutrients available in the food we have eaten.

The value of villi

Inside the villi there are tiny blood vessels called **capillaries**. The **vitamins** and nutrients from the digested food in the small intestine pass through the villi into these capillaries. The villi greatly increase the total area of the intestine walls, so many nutrients can be absorbed at a time. Once nutrients have passed into the blood, they can be carried around the body to where they are needed.

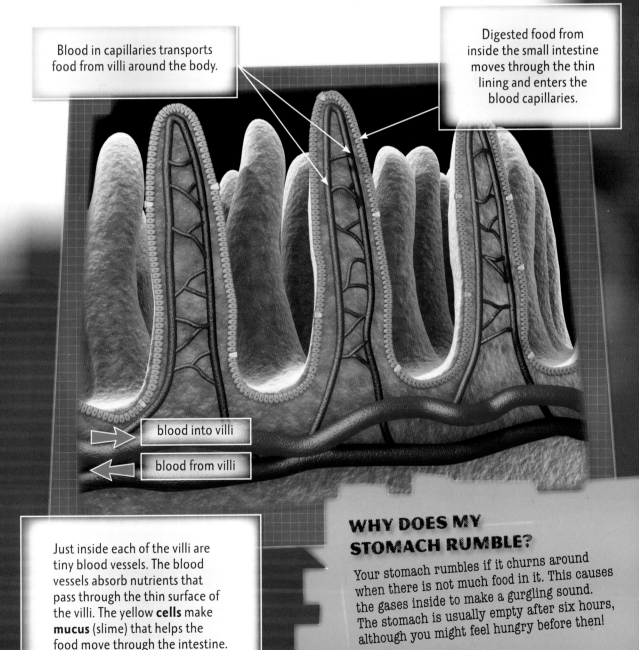

Blood in capillaries transports food from villi around the body.

Digested food from inside the small intestine moves through the thin lining and enters the blood capillaries.

blood into villi

blood from villi

Just inside each of the villi are tiny blood vessels. The blood vessels absorb nutrients that pass through the thin surface of the villi. The yellow **cells** make **mucus** (slime) that helps the food move through the intestine.

WHY DOES MY STOMACH RUMBLE?

Your stomach rumbles if it churns around when there is not much food in it. This causes the gases inside to make a gurgling sound. The stomach is usually empty after six hours, although you might feel hungry before then!

Aids to digestion

Food does not pass through the **liver**, **gall bladder**, or **pancreas** while it is being digested, but these organs are important tools in the digestive system. The liver and pancreas produce substances such as enzymes that help to break down food. The gall bladder acts as a storage warehouse for some of these substances.

The basics about bile

The liver is an organ about the width of your rib cage. One of its jobs is to produce **bile**. Bile is a greenish-yellow digestive juice that helps to break up fatty foods. The liver stores the bile in the gall bladder, a pear-shaped organ found just below the liver. When the body needs bile for digestion—for example, after you have eaten—the gall bladder squirts some into the small intestine.

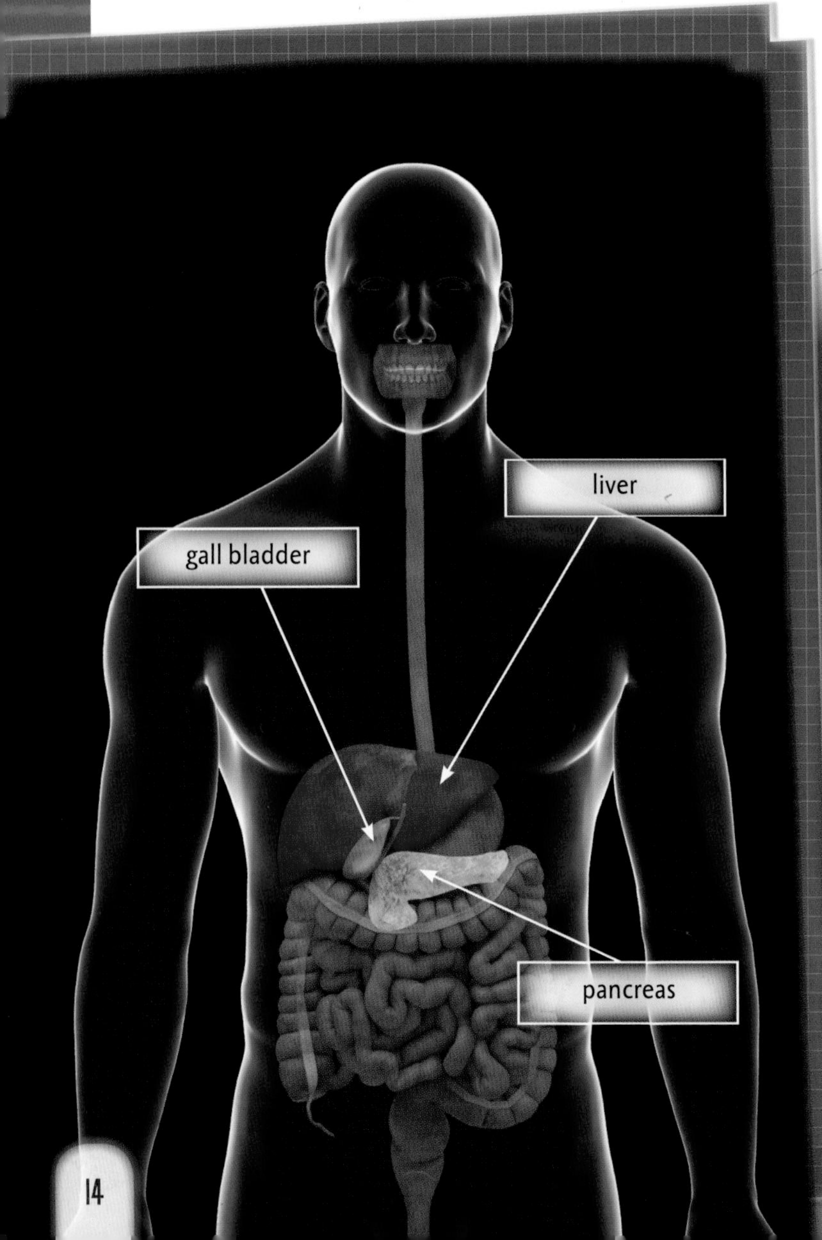

liver

gall bladder

pancreas

The liver, pancreas, and gall bladder supply the small intestine with the liquids it needs to digest food fully.

Pancreatic juice

The pancreas is about 7 inches (18 centimeters) long and lies behind and just below the stomach. The pancreas makes pancreatic juice. When you eat, your pancreas releases this juice into the first part of your small intestine. The fluid contains enzymes that break down fats, proteins, and carbohydrates.

When you wash the dishes, soap and detergent change oily food into tiny droplets that can be broken down and washed away more easily. Bile works on fatty food in a similar way.

WHY DO PEOPLE VOMIT?

If you have harmful bacteria in your stomach or intestine when you are sick, or you eat food with lots of strong chemicals in it, you may vomit to get rid of it. The muscles in your stomach and intestines automatically push the food up your esophagus and out of your mouth. Vomit usually tastes bitter, because it contains bile and gastric juices.

How Does the Body Use Food?

From the villi, blood carries nutrients to the liver through tubes called blood vessels. The liver is the largest organ inside your body, and it works like a chemical-processing factory.

Life in the liver

After a meal, the liver sorts out the nutrients. It converts useful nutrients into substances your body can use to make the energy it needs. The liver is also a storage depot. It holds on to nutrients and vitamins until supplies get low. Then it releases them back into the blood to be distributed around the body. For example, your body cannot use all the glucose it produces at once, so the liver stores it as a substance called glycogen. The liver changes this back to glucose when the body needs it. It is similar to the way a battery stores energy, releasing it only when it is needed by an electrical machine.

When you use up a lot of energy, your liver releases nutrients into the blood so your body can make more energy.

At a waste recycling center, magnets sort out useful metals from waste materials. In the human machine, the liver sorts out the useful chemicals from the harmful or useless ones in blood.

Waste filter

Digested food also contains substances your body does not need. In addition to sorting and storing nutrients, the liver also acts as a waste disposal unit. It helps to clean the blood—for example, by turning harmful substances into bile. In total, an adult's liver dumps around 1 pint (half a liter) of bile into the gall bladder each day.

JAUNDICE

When people have jaundice, their eyes and skin look a bit yellow. This happens because there is a buildup of waste products such as bile in their blood. It is a sign that something is wrong with their liver. The liver is a vital organ, so a doctor should always check any sign of jaundice.

Delivery service

When the liver has sorted the digested food and disposed of the waste, the blood acts like a fleet of delivery trucks. It carries nutrients to all of the different living cells in your body. Each one of us is made up of hundreds of millions of cells, which is why cells are often called the building blocks of living things.

How do cells use nutrients?

The cells of the body use different nutrients in different ways. For example, during the process of digestion, proteins from foods such as milk and cheese are broken down into their separate parts, called amino acids. The cells combine these different amino acids in different ways to build new cells and to repair damaged ones. Most of the carbohydrates we digest form glucose, and cells use glucose to make energy.

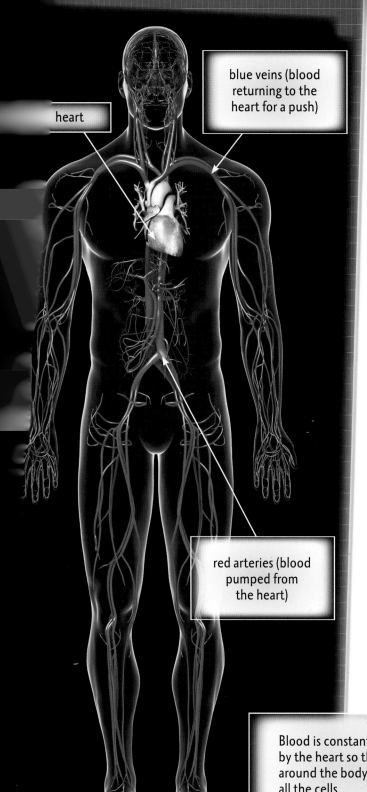

heart

blue veins (blood returning to the heart for a push)

red arteries (blood pumped from the heart)

Blood is constantly pumped by the heart so that it flows around the body to reach all the cells.

Collecting waste products

Complicated chemical reactions take place inside individual cells when they use up nutrients. These reactions produce some waste in the cells. For example, ammonia is the waste that is left over when cells use proteins to make new cells. Ammonia is toxic (poisonous) in large quantities. The blood carries ammonia away from the cells and back through the circulation system until it reaches the liver. The liver then changes the ammonia into a different waste, called **urea**, that is less harmful to the body.

In some ways blood cells are like trucks on a winding system of roads. They travel around the body in blood vessels, dropping off nutrients to cells and collecting waste.

RELEASING ENERGY

Inside individual cells, oxygen combines with glucose in a special reaction to release energy. Any substance that combines with oxygen to release heat energy is called a fuel. In a bonfire the fuel is wood, but in a cell it is glucose. In a cell there are no flames, as in a bonfire, but some heat is produced.

What Happens to Food Waste?

Kidneys are organs that are part of the body's waste disposal, or excretory, system. We have two kidneys, each about the size of a fist and shaped like a kidney bean. When blood passes through the kidneys, the kidneys remove excess water and waste products from the blood. The kidneys work fast—all of the blood in your body passes through your kidneys in four minutes.

How do kidneys work?

Uncleaned blood comes into each kidney through a large blood vessel. Kidneys work by filtering or straining waste from the blood. The filtering units inside the kidneys are called nephrons. Nephrons are like tiny tubes, and each kidney has a million of them! After waste has been removed, the cleaned blood leaves the kidney and re-enters the circulation system.

A coffee machine removes the unwanted grounds of coffee from the liquid. The kidneys remove unwanted waste from the blood in a similar way.

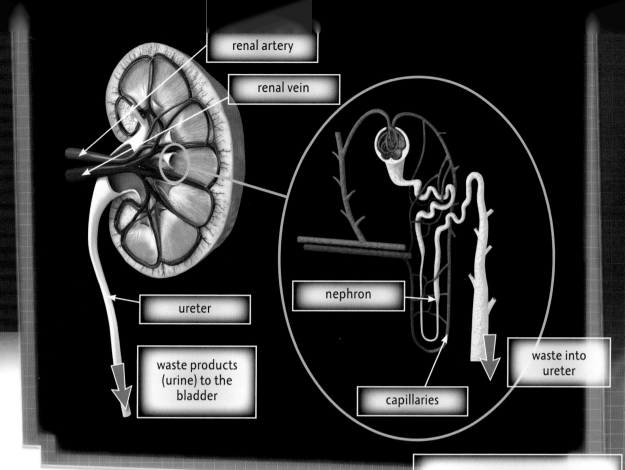

renal artery

renal vein

nephron

ureter

waste into
ureter

waste products
(urine) to the
bladder

capillaries

Filtering fluids

A tiny blood vessel called a capillary winds
around the inside of each of the cup-shaped
nephrons in a kidney. As blood passes through
each capillary, waste and some useful substances
filter into the nephron. Nutrients such as glucose
then move back into the capillary, along with
most of the water. These vital substances
flow on through the capillaries,
to the renal vein, and out of
the kidney.

In this picture the dirty
blood entering the kidney
is colored red. The cleaned
blood, leaving the kidney
through the renal vein, is
colored blue.

WHAT IS DIALYSIS?

When a person's kidneys are damaged,
a dialysis machine can be used to clean
the blood and remove waste and excess
water. A dialysis machine filters blood using
an artificial filter. A tube is attached to
a needle that has been inserted into a blood
vessel in the arm. Blood travels from the
body to the machine, is cleaned, and then
returns to the body through a second tube.

Waste disposal

The kidneys combine the different waste collected by the nephrons, such as urea, with excess water from the blood. This forms urine. Urine trickles out of the kidneys through two narrow tubes called ureters and passes into the bladder.

What is the bladder?

The bladder is a stretchy pouch that is used as a storage tank for urine. When it is empty, the bladder has many folds. These folds open up and flatten out as the bladder fills up, allowing it to expand. An adult bladder can usually hold about 1 pint (half a liter) before it feels uncomfortable. Urine leaves the body by flowing out of the bladder and down a tube called the urethra. The urethral sphincter is a ring of muscle at the point where the bladder and urethra meet. It is usually closed to hold urine in the bladder.

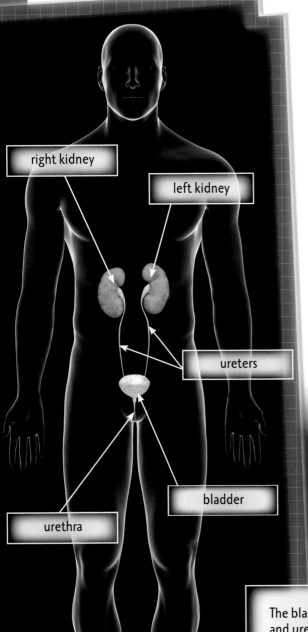

right kidney

left kidney

ureters

bladder

urethra

The bladder, urethra, and ureters are the main organs of liquid excretion.

How does the bladder work?

When the bladder is stretched to a certain point—usually about half full—**nerves** in the bladder wall send a message to the brain telling it that the bladder needs emptying. Nerves are like telephone wires inside the human body. They carry messages to and from the brain. The brain sends a message back, telling the body it is time to urinate. When you are ready, you relax the sphincter, and urine flows down the urethra and out of your body.

We also get rid of some waste when we sweat. Sweat helps us cool down, and it also releases small amounts of the waste that is carried by the blood.

WHAT IS SWEAT?

We sweat to cool down. When sweat dries from our body, it takes away some of the warmth, too. Sweat also helps to carry waste from the body. Although it consists mostly of water, sweat also contains some urea and salt that is filtered from the blood as the blood travels under the skin.

Solid waste

Some of the materials in food cannot be digested in the small intestine. For example, some parts of fruits and vegetables are made of **fiber**, a tough substance that does not contain any nutrients. Fiber, other bits of undigested food, and used bile pass straight from the small intestine into the large intestine.

In the large intestine

The large intestine, or bowel, is made up of three sections: the colon, rectum, and anus. The first and largest part is the colon. Undigested food stays in the colon for up to 24 hours. During this time most of the remaining water is removed from the waste. The semi-solid waste that is left over is called feces.

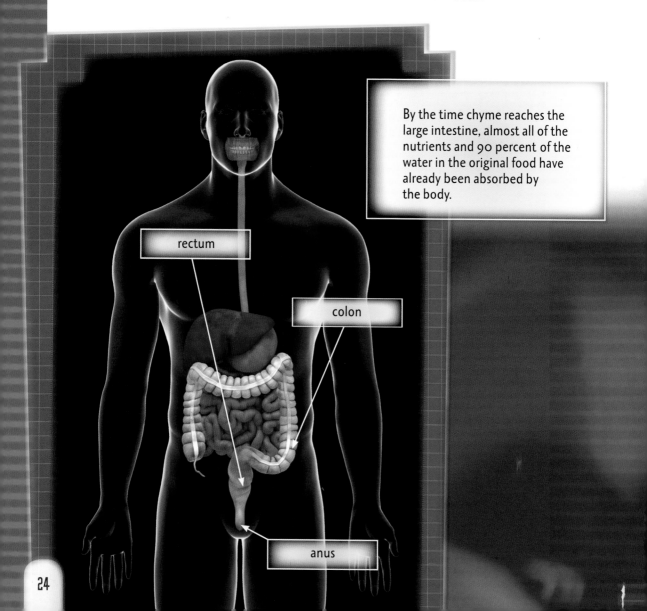

By the time chyme reaches the large intestine, almost all of the nutrients and 90 percent of the water in the original food have already been absorbed by the body.

rectum

colon

anus

Dumping the waste

Some bacteria normally live in the colon. They break down some of the fiber to nourish themselves. This makes the feces easier to get rid of. Mucus made by cells lining the colon help the feces slip through the colon into the rectum. Feces are stored in the rectum until we are ready to pass them out in stools, which leave the body through the anus.

We sometimes also pass gas from the anus. This gas is created in the alimentary canal when food is broken down and when bacteria in the colon break down undigested fiber.

Many yogurts contain probiotics. Probiotics can help keep our digestive system, particularly the large intestine, healthy.

FRIENDLY BACTERIA?

There is a mix of healthy and harmful bacteria in your colon. Many doctors suggest eating foods such as yogurt that contain probiotics. These are healthy or "friendly" bacteria. They help maintain a healthy colon by increasing the numbers of helpful bacteria there.

How Can We Keep the Digestive System Healthy?

To keep your digestive system healthy, you need to eat a balance of healthy foods and drink plenty of water. Your body is mostly made of water, and water keeps food moving through the digestive system smoothly. You lose water every day, through sweat and urination, and it is important to replace that supply.

Different food groups

You need to eat food from different food groups. Fruits and vegetables, and grains such as rice or wheat, supply us with carbohydrates and also with much of the fiber and vitamins we need. Try to eat at least five portions of fruits or vegetables each day.

Carbohydrates in cereals, bread, potatoes, or pasta made from grains take longer to digest than those in sweet foods. They therefore release energy gradually and let us remain active over a long time. So fill up on the right carbohydrates at mealtimes and not on cookies or cakes in between.

Wholemeal carbohydrates like this loaf of bread contain lots of fiber. Fiber keeps our digestive system healthy by helping to push waste through the alimentary canal.

You should try to eat a portion of protein with at least two of your main meals each day. Protein is found in meat, fish, and pulses (seeds) such as lentils. The other food groups are dairy foods such as milk and cheese, and oily foods such as nuts and seeds. These supply some protein, but mostly fat. This nutrient is important for keeping us healthy, but in large amounts it can make us overweight and unfit.

Minerals, such as calcium and iron, are also very important for your health. For example, calcium builds strong bones and teeth. You should get the minerals you need by eating different foods from all food groups.

You can help your digestive system by eating healthy foods in the correct amount and also by washing your hands to keep germs out.

WHY SHOULD I WASH MY HANDS?

It is especially important to wash your hands with warm, soapy water after going to the bathroom, because you may have traces of feces or urine on your fingers. If the bacteria in these waste substances get into your mouth and back into your system, they could make you sick.

The World's Most Complex Machine

The human body is often described as the world's most complex machine, but of course it is not really a machine at all. Machines are non-living, mechanical objects, whereas our bodies are natural, living things. But there are similarities. Like a machine, the body is made up of different parts that work together in systems to do particular jobs. These different systems work together to make the whole body—or the human machine—run smoothly and efficiently.

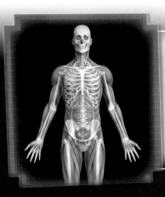

THE SKELETAL SYSTEM

This system of bones supports the other parts of the body, rather like the way the metal frame of a car supports the vehicle.

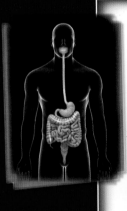

THE DIGESTIVE SYSTEM

The digestive system works as a food-processing machine. It consists of various organs that work together to break down food into forms that the body can use as fuel and raw materials.

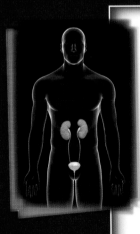

THE EXCRETORY SYSTEM

This is the human machine's waste disposal system, removing harmful substances and waste produced by the other parts of the body.

THE NERVOUS SYSTEM

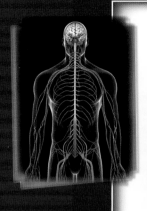

This is the human machine's communication and control system. The brain transmits and receives messages from the senses and the rest of the body. It does this through a network of nerves connected to the brain via the spinal cord.

THE CIRCULATORY SYSTEM

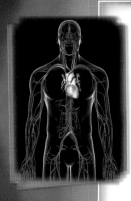

This is the body's delivery system. The heart pumps blood through blood vessels, carrying nutrients and oxygen to the other parts and removing waste from cells.

THE RESPIRATORY SYSTEM

This system provides the rest of the body with the oxygen it needs to get energy from food. It also releases waste gases from the body into the air.

THE MUSCULAR SYSTEM

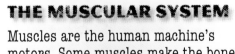

Muscles are the human machine's motors. Some muscles make the bones of the skeleton move, while others work as pumps to keep substances moving through the body.

Glossary

acid type of substance. Mild acids such as lemon juice taste sharp, but strong acids, such as the acid made in our stomach, damage or break down other substances.

alimentary canal passage that food moves along during digestion, from mouth to anus

anus hole at the end of the large intestine through which waste solids and gas leave the body

bacteria microscopic living thing. Some bacteria can cause disease.

bile digestive juice made by the liver that digests fat in the small intestine

capillary smallest kind of blood vessel in the body

carbohydrate kind of food such as pasta, bread, and potatoes that gives us energy

cell building block or basic unit of all living things. The human body is made up of millions of different cells.

chyme paste of partly digested food in the stomach

digest break down foods we eat

dissolve disintegrate or disappear into a liquid such as water

energy in science, energy is the ability to do work—to move, grow, change, or to do anything else that living things do

enzyme special protein that helps body processes, including digestion

epiglottis flap behind the tongue that stops food from going toward the lungs as you swallow

esophagus tube between the throat and stomach

excrete force out waste

fiber tough substance, found in some foods, that the body cannot digest

gall bladder pouch near the liver that stores bile

glucose kind of sugar that the body obtains from carbohydrate foods such as pasta and potatoes

kidney organ that filters waste from the blood and forms urine

large intestine (also called the bowel) part of the alimentary tract, made up of the colon, rectum, and anus

liver large organ that removes and stores nutrients and converts some waste in the blood into bile

lungs organs we use to breathe

microscopic substance so small that you need a microscope to see it

mineral non-living substance such as metal, salt, sand, or calcium. Minerals often come from the earth.

mucus slimy substance made by some cells. Mucus is found throughout the alimentary canal.

muscle tissue in the body that contracts (tightens) to cause movement

muscular made of muscle

nerve thin strand that carries messages between the brain and the rest of the body

nutrient substance that plants and animals need to grow and survive

organ part of the body that performs a specific function

pancreas organ that makes the enzymes used in digestion

protein type of nutrient found in foods. Meat is a protein and is very important for the growth and repair of the body.

small intestine part of the alimentary canal between the stomach and large intestine

urea waste product created by the liver after cells use up proteins

villi tiny finger-shaped folds inside the small intestine

vitamin important nutrients released after our bodies digest foods such as fruits and vegetables

Find Out More

Websites

At www.kidshealth.org/kid/body/digest_SW.html you will find "The Real Deal on the Digestive System." The "KidsHealth" website also has useful sections on nutrients and many different human body topics.

At http://exhibits.pacsci.org/nutrition/nutrition_cafe.html you can learn more about eating the right foods to stay healthy. Try playing some games.

At http://vilenski.org/science/humanbody/hb_html/digestivesystem.html you can view the digestive system as part of the "Human Body Adventure." Click to see close-up views of different parts of the digestive system.

Books

Glass, Susan. *The Human Body: The Digestive System*. Logan, Iowa: Perfection Learning, 2004.

Parker, Steve. *Digestion*. Chicago: Raintree, 2004.

Sheen, Barbara. *Eating Right*. Chicago: Heinemann Library, 2008.

Simon, Seymour. *Guts: Our Digestive System*. New York: Harper Collins, 2005.

Index